COLOURFUL
SCOTLAND

Lomond Books

This edition published in 1997 by Lomond Books,
36 West Shore Road, Granton, Edinburgh EH5 1QD

© 1984 Coombe Books

Printed in China

ISBN 1–85833–721–6

Scotland is a land of perpetual mystery and enchantment, where the wealth of history and tradition combine with a modern urge and outlook to give an air of magic and excitement unique to the country. A lonely road across the Highlands stretches away over the windswept mountains and the clachans are beacons of warmth and shelter in a desolate landscape. The kingdom is a land where the tide of human emotions has run at its strongest. Claymores and broadswords have been taken to battle by men with revenge in their hearts, and the mists of Glencoe still weep for the MacDonald dead.

But such bloody matters seem a thousand miles from the peaceful Western Isles. Set in a gleaming sea, the dark islands stand like sentinels in the Atlantic. Rising above the long, deep inlets are the heather-covered hills where graze the sheep which produce the wool for the famous Harris tweed. With names like Benbecula and Taransay, the islands are the last bastions of the Gaelic language and culture whose legacy still pervades the Highlands. The small fishing villages lie clustered about the inlets; home to the trawlers that brave the mighty ocean. But the islands are not always so peaceful and calm. During the winter savage storms will sweep the coasts, pounding against the rocks and sending spray high into the wind-wrenched air.

Across the shining Minch, which lies protected behind the wild outer islands, is the almost legendary Isle of Skye. Amidst the scenery of wind-blown heather rise the towers of Dunvegan Castle, where are housed the tattered remains of the Fairy Flag, given to a long dead Macleod of Macleod by his fairy wife. It was to these wild shores and towering mountains that Bonny Prince Charlie came in 1746, after the crushing defeat of his clans at Culloden. After many weeks hiding among the beautiful islands and glens that could never be his, the Prince fled to France, never to return.

As the dark, rolling hills and moors stretch away northwards to the Pentland Firth, the endless vista of bare rock and marshy hollow combine with the howling wind to create an air of wild beauty that cannot be matched anywhere else. The heather-covered hillsides are rich with life. Red deer and grouse are the favourite prey of the hunters who come to these hills during the season. One of the great delights of the Highlands is to tramp for miles across the awe-inspiring landscape, be it in sunshine or in drizzle, and to return to a fireside and a good meal. It is easy to see the magical quality that turns Scottish hearts to the Highlands. Though the bens and glens have seen more than their share of clan feuding and bloodshed, they are now at peace and the great hills are dotted with sheep and trees. But as the gleaming streams wind amongst the heather and the savage wind whips the grass, it is almost as if the plaid-clad men of the past can be seen on their way to wreak vengeance on a neighbouring clan. The majestic scenery of the northern Highlands stretches from Cape Wrath southwards until it is cut short by the Great Glen.

This deep valley slices across the Highlands like a sixty-mile-long sword-cut. The result of great geological forces, this valley runs from Inverness to Fort William and has rightly been called the greatest feature of the Highlands. In its gloomy depths can be found the brooding waters of Loch Ness. Though a great beauty spot and a fine fishing ground, the loch is chiefly known for its monster, hunted in vain by scientists from around the world. On the south side of the glen the land rises again to form the Cairngorm and Grampian Mountains, which are grander than their counterparts on the other side of the Great Glen. These giants are even more impressive when compared to the tiny houses and castles that find shelter beneath the peaks. One of the many homes nestled amid the awesome grandeur is the castle of Balmoral, the favourite Scottish retreat of the Royal Family for well over a century. As well as sheltering the castle of Balmoral, these snowcapped peaks rise above the greatest treasures of Scotland; her distilleries. From these hidden glens and tiny burns the precious amber liquid flows out to all corners of the world, bringing jollity and comradeship to many a lonely heart.

Along the east coast of the Highlands are found the many ports whose fishing fleets set out into the treacherous North Sea in search of herring and mackerel. Aberdeen, Stonehaven and Arbroath may be the largest, but it is Montrose that lives in history. It was James Graham, the Marquess of Montrose, who raised the standard for King Charles in Scotland and won a series of victories against Parliament.

Leaving the dramatic scenery of the desolate Highlands to the north, the rich Lowlands stretch out to the south. Here is found the agricultural wealth of the nation; sheep, cattle and wheat are produced in abundance. The soft beauty of the fertile land is in sharp contrast to the wild grandeur of the mountains and the glens. The rolling agricultural land is suddenly interrupted by the rocky crag at Stirling. Perched on this rocky height, the castle is the centre of the city which lies huddled around its base for protection from the dangers of war. Further down the silvery waters of the Firth of Forth lies the great capital of Scotland; Edinburgh. Standing alone on its rock, the ancient fortress of Edinburgh Castle proudly towers above the city. For centuries it has stood, the centre and focus of history, be it bloody or romantic. The view across the city from the Castle to Palace of Holyroodhouse is truly remarkable, taking in the Royal Mile and the beauties of the 'Athens of the North'. To the west of Edinburgh, on the Clyde, can be found the great industrial heart of the nation. The city of Glasgow spreads out from the river in a mass of business and industrial areas which have made Scotland the nation she is today. But still the heart of every Scot is in the Highlands amid the heather and the tartan.

(Left) Dunbar Harbour and Castle.

(Opposite page) part of the fishing fleet of Pittenweem. An Augustinian priory was founded here in 1141 and, near the harbour, is the cave-shrine of St Fillan. (This page, far left) sunset over Loch Laggan. (Left) Ben Nevis, the highest mountain in Great Britain at 4,406 ft, seen across the head of Loch Linnhe. (Below) the bay at Morar, famous for its white sands. (Bottom) Loch Katrine's Ellen's Isle features in Sir Walter Scott's *The Lady of the Lake*.

(This page, right) the ruin of Lochranza Castle, which dates from the 16th century, on the Isle of Arran. Its walls overlook Loch Ranza on whose shores, in 1306, Robert the Bruce is believed to have landed from Ireland. He went on to seize the Scottish throne that year, and spent years harrying English forces in his country, eventually defeating them in a set-piece battle at Bannockburn in 1314. He secured English recognition of Scotland's independence by the Treaty of Northampton in 1328. (Below) the sun's rays stream over the peak of Blaven on the Isle of Skye. In the Highland region lies Eilean Donan Castle (opposite page, top) and the crofting and fishing villages of Shieldaig (bottom left) and Plockton (bottom right).

(Opposite page) the River Dochart and (bottom) seen as it flows past Killin. The village overlooks Loch Tay, at the head of which lie the ruins of Finlarig Castle, where can be seen perhaps the only remaining example of an ancient beheading pit. The castle is described in Sir Walter Scott's 1828 novel *The Fair Maid of Perth*. (This page, far left) the hay lies harvested in the fields, ready to be stored when dry for winter feeding, whilst the sheep (left) enjoy the verdant, sun-swept pasture. (Below) springtime at Finstown on the Bay of Firth, Mainland; the largest of over 70 islands in the Orkney group.

(Opposite page and this page, top) the 'Fair City' of Perth, capital of Scotland for a century until 1437, lies at the head of the estuary of the River Tay. (Right) the river seen from Kinnoull Hill. (Above centre) Drummond Castle, near Crieff, was once bombarded by the cannon of Cromwell. (Above) part of the world-famous Gleneagles golf course.

(Opposite page, top) the Caledonian Canal and Ben Nevis and (bottom) the waterway seen at Corpach. The canal (this page, top right and centre left) runs along the Great Glen, connecting several lochs including Loch Linnhe (top left). (Left) Loch Leven and the Glenduror Heights. (Above) the Crinan Canal was built in 1793-1801 so that ships could reach the Atlantic from Loch Fyne, avoiding sailing south.

(Opposite page, centre left) Loch Eil; (bottom right) Glen Orchy. (Remaining pictures) Glencoe, which means the 'glen of weeping' in Gaelic, was the scene of the treacherous attack upon the Macdonalds by men under the control of Archibald Campbell, the 10th Earl of Argyll. When King James II was replaced on the throne by William of Orange in 1689, many clans stayed loyal to James. So, in August 1691, the government offered indemnity to all chiefs who swore allegiance before 1st January, 1692. The chiefs accepted, but brave Alexander Macdonald decided to leave his oath-taking until 31st December, 1691, the day before the deadline. When it was discovered that there was no magistrate in Fort William to take his oath, it was delayed until the 6th. By way of dire example, 100 soldiers made welcome by the Macdonalds for over a week, suddenly attacked their hosts on 13th February; 38 were slaughtered, including the chief; others died later in the snow.

(These pages) Edinburgh. (Above) the Scott Monument in Princes Street Gardens. Pipers (below and opposite page) and (right) at the Military Tatoo. (Bottom right) memorial to the Royal Scots Greys.

(This page, top) Loch Ard lies within the Queen Elizabeth Forest Park. (Right) Loch Affric, near Cannich. (Below) Loch Awe and Kilchurn Castle, held by Lord Breadalbane during the '45 to prevent the Jacobites marching south by this route. (Opposite page, top left) Glen Clova and the Grampians. (Top right) the Lochan Fada. (Bottom) the River Leny at Callander, north of Stirling.

(Opposite page and this page, bottom right) the harbour of Pittenweem. (Left) the luxury liner *Queen Elizabeth II* sails past Cloch Point, in the outer reaches of the Clyde estuary, where stands a lighthouse built in 1797. Facing it stands the resort of Dunoon. The ship, used to carry soldiers during the Falklands Campaign, was built on Clydeside and launched in September 1967. (Below) Easdale. (Bottom left) Anstruther.

(This page, top) Loch Moy. Nearby, the 'Rout of Moy' took place during the '45, when men under Lord Loudoun's command fled in disarray. (Above) Loch Garry. (Right) Loch Ness, whose monster was first seen by St Columba in AD 565. (Opposite page, top) Loch Eil. (Bottom) Loch Tummel.

(This page, top) the lighthouse at Cantick Head. (Right) Badcall. (Below) the Stacks of Duncansby lie off the coast near John O' Groats (opposite page, top). (Bottom left) Blair Castle is said to have been the last in Britain to withstand siege. (Bottom right) Dunbeath Castle.

(This page, right) Loch Ainort on the Isle of Skye. (Far right) Urquhart Castle, overlooking Loch Ness, raised by the Lords of the Isles, was sacked by Edward I. Robert the Bruce lay siege to and held the castle. It was blown up in 1692 to prevent its occupation by Jacobites. (Below) Loch Tummel seen from Queen's View. (Bottom left) Loch Eilt, which is bordered by the famous Road to the Isles. (Bottom right) Castle Stalker, which dates from about 1500, is associated with James IV, and the Royal Coat of Arms is carved over the entrance. (Opposite page) Loch Creran.

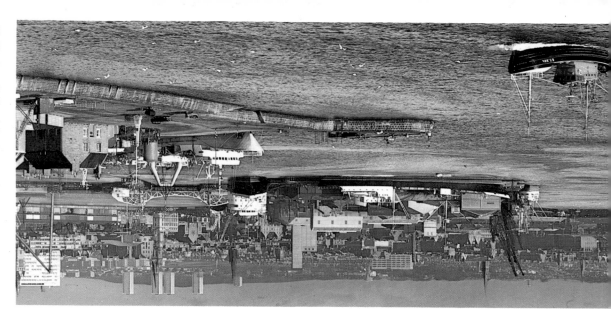

(These pages) Aberdeen, an important university and maritime city, lies on the estuaries of the Rivers Dee and Don. The charters for the city date back to about 1179. Edward I came to Aberdeen in 1296 and, after a battle in Methven Wood in 1306, Robert the Bruce did too. The city's motto, *Bon Accord*, was the rallying cry of the Bruces. Edward III burnt the city in 1337 and Montrose occupied the city three times. Today, the Municipal Buildings incorporate the Old Tolbooth, scene of public executions until 1857, which preserves the 'Aberdeen Maiden' – the instrument on which the French guillotine was modelled.

(This page, top) the magnificent, rugged peaks of the Cuillins of Skye. (Above) Stromness, Orkney Islands, looks across Hoy Sound and southeast to Scapa Flow, the former base of the Grand Fleet. (Right) Strath Mashie. (Opposite page, top) Lerwick, Shetland Islands. King Haco of Norway came to the harbour in 1263, before the Battle of Largs. (Bottom) Skara Brae, Mainland, in the Orkney Islands, is a Stone Age village still remaining in a good state of preservation.

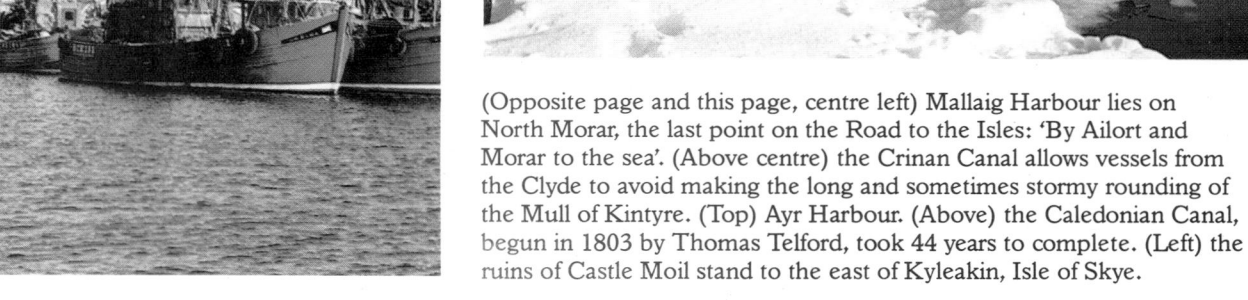

(Opposite page and this page, centre left) Mallaig Harbour lies on North Morar, the last point on the Road to the Isles: 'By Ailort and Morar to the sea'. (Above centre) the Crinan Canal allows vessels from the Clyde to avoid making the long and sometimes stormy rounding of the Mull of Kintyre. (Top) Ayr Harbour. (Above) the Caledonian Canal, begun in 1803 by Thomas Telford, took 44 years to complete. (Left) the ruins of Castle Moil stand to the east of Kyleakin, Isle of Skye.

(These pages) Scotland, land of the claymore, clansmen warriors and castle keeps. (Right) Castle Stalker and (above and opposite page, top right) Eilean Donan Castle. (Left) Inverlochy Castle by Ben Nevis. (Bottom right) next to Loch Awe lies Kilchurn Castle, built in 1440, of which Wordsworth wrote, 'Child of loud-throated War! the mountain-stream roars in thy hearing; but thy hour of rest is come, and thou art silent in thy age'.

(Opposite page, top) haunted, 17th-century Glamis Castle, where the Old Pretender sojourned in 1715. (Centre left) Stirling Castle, recaptured from the English by Wallace in 1297, it was lost again in 1304 following a siege by Edward I. General Monk succeeded in taking the castle in 1651, but Prince Charles Edward failed in 1746. (Centre right) Urquhart Castle stands above Loch Ness. (Bottom left) Inverary Castle, on the shores of Loch Fyne, is the seat of the Duke of Argyll, head of Clan Campbell. (Bottom right) Balmoral Castle, the Queen's Highland home. (This page, top) the keep of Kilchurn Castle at Loch Awe was built in 1440 by Sir Colin Campbell, founder of the family of Breadalbane. (Left) the castle of Eilean Donan, whose name commemorates Saint Donan of Eigg, murdered by Norsemen.

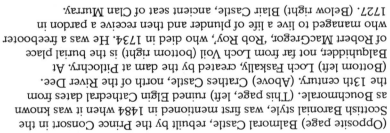

(Opposite page) Balmoral Castle, rebuilt by the Prince Consort in the Scottish Baronial style, was first mentioned in 1484 when it was known as Bouchmorale. (This page, left) ruined Elgin Cathedral dates from the 13th century. (Above) Crathes Castle, north of the River Dee. (Bottom left) Loch Faskally, created by the dam at Pitlochry. At Balquhidder, not far from Loch Voil (bottom right) is the burial place of Robert MacGregor, 'Rob Roy', who died in 1734. He was a freebooter who managed to live a life of plunder and then receive a pardon in 1727. (Below right) Blair Castle, ancient seat of Clan Murray.

(This page) St Andrews. (Far right) the square, 108-foot-high tower of the early-12th century St Rule's Church, now a ruin. In the cemetery nearby is buried Tom Morris (1821-1908), the famous golfer. (Right) the famous Road Hole, the Seventeenth, on the Old Course of The Royal and Ancient Golf Club of St Andrews (opposite page, top left), founded in 1754. (Bottom left) the cathedral in St Andrews was founded in 1160. King James V and Mary of Guise were married here and, in 1559, John Knox gave sermons within its walls. (Top right and bottom right) Crail and its harbour. (Centre right) St Monance.

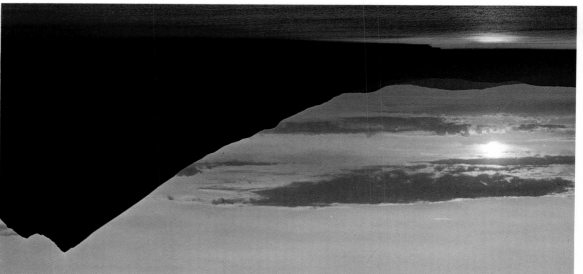

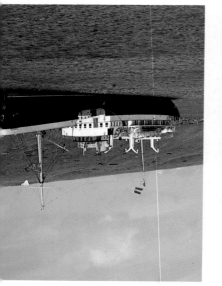

(This page, top left) the Bullers of Buchan is a 200-foot-deep chasm in the cliffs two miles northeast of Cruden Bay. (Top right) Scalloway lies west of Lerwick in the Shetland Islands. Nearby is Gallows Hill, where witches used to be burnt. (Centre right) a ship calls at Mid Yell, also in the Shetlands. (Above) sunset silhouettes Skye's Cuillin mountain ridge. (Right) the peak of Blaven which, at 3,042 feet, overlooks beautiful Loch na Creitheach. (Opposite page) St Margaret's Hope, on the northern coast of South Ronaldsay in the Orkney Islands, is linked by its name to Queen Margaret, the 'Maid of Norway', who died in 1290 on board a ship bound for Scotland.

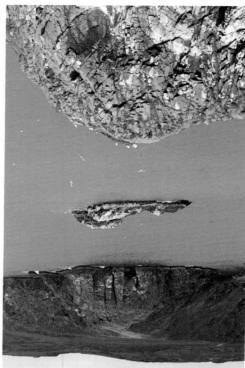

(Opposite page, top left and this page, left) the Isle of Mull. Dr Johnson visited the island in 1773 but his comment was, 'O Sir! a most dolorous country'. (Above, top and opposite page, top right) Oban Harbour is dominated by the large, circular stone structure known as McCaig's Folly. In the town, Dr Johnson and Boswell found themselves a 'tolerable' inn. (Bottom) the village of Findochty, between Long Head and Craig Head.

(Opposite page) Ben Nevis seen across the head of Loch Linnhe with Fort William on the far shore. (This page, far left) the twin Buchaille Etive peaks above the climbers' hut. (Left) a fine example of Highland cattle. (Below) Ben Nevis seen from Banavie. (Bottom left) erected in 1815 by Macdonald of Glenaladale, this monument commemorates Charles Edward Stuart's meeting with Lochiel and faithful supporters on 18th August, 1745. (Bottom right) the bagpipe's wail, sweet music of freedom echoing in the Highlands.

(Opposite page, top) Dundee seen from Newport-on-Tay with the Tay Road Bridge (centre left and right), completed in 1966, spanning the river's girth.
(Bottom left) spring flowers beside a burn in Aberfeldy. Here can be found the Black Watch Monument, erected in 1887 – Queen Victoria's Jubilee Year – to commemorate the founding of the regiment 150 years earlier.
(Bottom right) some 15 miles to the west of Perth lies the village of Crieff, Charles Edward Stuart, in 1746, held a council of war here in the 'Drummond Arms'. A few miles away is Drummond Castle. (This page, left) the Tay Road Bridge and (below) crossing the Firth of Tay are the new road bridge and the two-mile-long Tay Railway Bridge of 1887.

(This page, right) Loch Ness, famous for its monster, which can hide away in an estimated 263,000,000,000 cubic feet of water. (Below) near Spean Bridge is the bronze Commando Memorial, designed by Scott Sutherland in 1952, which commemorates those who trained here during World War II. (Bottom left) Loch Eil. (Bottom right) Castle Stalker. (Opposite page) Whiteness Voe.

(This page, top and right) Glasgow and the River Clyde. (Below) the Cross of Lorraine on Lyle Hill, Greenock, overlooking the Firth of Clyde, is a monument to Free French sailors who died in the Battle of the Atlantic. (Bottom right) the beautiful bay at Oban. (Opposite page, top) wharves beyond the River Clyde's Kingston Bridge. (Bottom left) Glasgow's 19th-century University Buildings with the City Chambers on George Square (bottom right).

(Opposite page, bottom) Dumfries on the banks of the River Nith, which is crossed by the 15th-century Old Bridge, used only as a footbridge today. Interesting places in the town include the Burns House, where Robert Burns died in 1796. On a building in Castle Street there is a plaque marking the place where, in 1306, Robert Bruce is said to have stabbed the 'Red Comyn' in the former Greyfriars monastery church. (Top) the Burns Monument seen from the Brig O'Doon, Alloway, and the statue (this page, below) are Ayr's tribute to the famous Scottish poet. (Far left) Kilchurn Castle, used as a garrison for Hanoverian soldiers in 1746. (Left) Blair Castle, Blair Atholl. The seat of the Duke of Atholl, head of Clan Murray, he has the rare privilege of being a British subject who is allowed to have his own private army, the Atholl Highlanders.

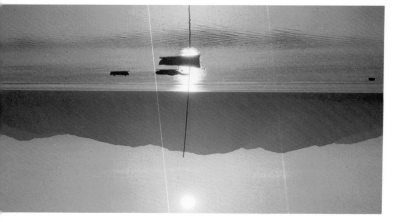

(This page, above) Port of Menteith. (Right) Loch Garten. The schooner *Captain Scott* (below) on Loch Eil (below right). (Bottom) Largs where, in 1263, King Haco of Norway was defeated in battle. (Opposite page) the Glendaruel Heights across Loch Leven. (Overleaf) Loch Shiel and Prince Charles Edward monument.